THE TREMBLING ANSWERS

BOA wishes to acknowledge the generosity of the following
40 for 40 Major Gift Donors

Lannan Foundation
Gouvernet Arts Fund
Angela Bonazinga & Catherine Lewis
Boo Poulin

CRAIG MORGAN TEICHER

THE TREMBLING ANSWERS

POEMS

AMERICAN POETS CONTINUUM SERIES, No. 160

BOA EDITIONS, LTD. ◨ ROCHESTER, NY ◨ 2017

First Edition

18 19 20 21 7 6 5 4 3

For information about permission to reuse any material from this book, please contact The Permissions Company at www.permissionscompany.com or e-mail perm-dude@gmail.com.

Publications by BOA Editions, Ltd.—a not-for-profit corporation under section 501 (c) (3) of the United States Internal Revenue Code—are made possible with funds from a variety of sources, including public funds from the Literature Program of the National Endowment for the Arts; the New York State Council on the Arts, a state agency; and the County of Monroe, NY. Private funding sources include the Lannan Foundation for support of the Lannan Translations Selection Series; the Max and Marian Farash Charitable Foundation; the Mary S. Mulligan Charitable Trust; the Rochester AreaCommunity Foundation; the Steeple-Jack Fund; the Ames-Amzalak Memorial Trust in memory of Henry Ames, Semon Amzalak, and Dan Amzalak; and contributions from many individuals nationwide. See Colophon on page 88 for special individual acknowledgments.

ART WORKS.
arts.gov

State of the Arts

NYSCA

Cover Design: Sandy Knight
Interior Design and Composition: Richard Foerster
Manufacturing: Bookmobile
BOA Logo: Mirko

Library of Congress Cataloging-in-Publication Data

Names: Teicher, Craig Morgan, 1979– author.
Title: The trembling answers : poems / by Craig Morgan Teicher.
Description: First edition. | Rochester, NY : BOA Editions Ltd., [2017] |
   Series: American poets continuum ; 160
Identifiers: LCCN 2016045572| ISBN 9781942683315 (paperback : alk. paper) |
   ISBN 9781942683322 (ebook)
Subjects: | BISAC: POETRY / American / General. | FAMILY & RELATIONSHIPS
   / Children with Special Needs. | FAMILY & RELATIONSHIPS / Parenting /
   Fatherhood.
Classification: LCC PS3620.E4359 A6 2017 | DDC 811/.6—dc23
LC record available at https://lccn.loc.gov/2016045572

BOA Editions, Ltd.
250 North Goodman Street, Suite 306
Rochester, NY 14607
www.boaeditions.org
A. Poulin, Jr., Founder (1938–1996)

For Simone

Contents

ONE

Every Turning

Every turning toward is a turning away:
poets have always known the truth
of this. I read
my book because

time in my home is senseless and
unbearable. I shower so as not
to have to face
the inevitable

crackling of my focus when I read,
and I binge-watch *The Blacklist*
to forestall the
interminable

chore post-shower of drying
my desperate and overgrown
hair, having also
forestalled

my annual haircut, which I refuse
to attend to daily because
I am handsome
if I avoid

the mirror. But of course none
of this is what I am truly
avoiding. Death
is shorthand

for *Death*, for life's uncountable
endings and its ultra-vivid
catalog of things
undone, hopes

unfulfilled, opportunities unnoticed so
untaken. I could cite lips not kissed
or kissed once and never again;
high school nights

spent grieving high school nights—they stick
in the heart like sharp bones,
clog the way like
artery-fat;

instruments never learned—my dream
of playing piano is already
impossible, as is
my wise plan never

to fall prey to credit card debt.
But, obviously, I mean something
deeper, an avoidance
more futile and

tragic, so primary and unnameable
I shall be forced to talk around it
—say everything but—
all my droning, hasty

years: not death but what it surrounds,
this one life that is all that I am,
prize I fail
to value

because I mistake it for a consolation against
the sting of some other, greater loss.
Birdsong, sunset, music unfolding
in and out of time,

the taste of chocolate blossoming so generously
across my tongue, my daughter laughing,
my sighing son,
warming winter air,

waking unworried from a weird, good dream,
thousands of orgasms, tongue and thigh
and arch, a clean room,
alphabetized

books on shelf after happy shelf, drunkenness,
sleep, crying out and crying over
my pain, my wondrous
pain.

Self-Portrait Beside Myself

We've been lucky—March is over
and my son is still alive. My daughter
is about to crawl. And the golden
sunset light recalls
distant childhood light.
I feed my son while he sleeps
through a hole in his tummy
when the night nurse
has the night off,
and when I go to the mirror
it's to see if the ocean-eyed man
the teenager I was had hoped to become
is anywhere in there.
The teenager is; he wants you
to see him, help him, tell him
he's strong and gently
dramatic. He wants
to be part of a story, even
if not a true one. He wants
to fuck like mad,
even if I don't. Standing over my son
at night, I feel quiet, only then,
no need to be me or anyone,
just listening to him breathe.
I can divide all life
into breath and waiting
for the next breath, and
the calm in the troughs
between. I wanted
to show you I could see the world
without me in the way; I can't, not
even for a little while. I'm beside
that man watching over his son,
impressed with him and his humility.

But if that's what it takes,
to keep my son safe—admiring
my better self rather than
being him—then ok. That's ok.

Free

I'm free as long as I have
this cigar clenched between
my teeth, sitting out front,
the baby monitor bringing

the sounds of heartbeat
and breath as far as the
tether will stretch. I'm free
to think what I'd like, beholden

to no one in my silence.
I'm so free I'm almost not
even me, and the voice
in my head could be anyone's.

Now a golden cat runs by—free.

But why begin with the cigar,
its foul smoke, with my
teeth, chipped as they never
were when I was beautiful?

Because these are the facts, the
few clear facts: my teeth,
my teeth are yellowing
in my mouth all the time.

My thick, weird tongue
licks at the tarred, rolled
leaves and is blistered and
burned. These are among

the truths it's been given me
to tell. I'm free to tell them,

scrunched like a toad in my
head. I've not showered in

days; my hair is waxy. What
a beautiful sentence, its
perfectly placed semicolon
a reminder of all I can hope

to accomplish. I'm free
to stink of tobacco and sweat
and free to tell anyone
who cares to know: *Craig*

Morgan Teicher sits outside
of his apartment tonight!
Do you hear me? I'm outside and
nothing will ever make me go in!

Night Nurse

Lately we invite this stranger into our home
to watch over, like an angel or good dog,

                         our son.

But she is not angelic, not graceful, her slippers
flopping like sad clown shoes. And it's wrong

to compare this nurse to a dog, especially
that kind of dog: trusted, beloved. We need her

so we hate her, even though it is—must be—our fault
she's here
          —he is *our* son—
                   so we give

instructions and thanks before quarantining
in our room
                where we sourly purse our eyes

toward sleep while she is paid
                   to guard our son against
that more familiar stranger, who should have

no business with a child,
                not now, not here. But endings
are always near. Passing our door, her steps

sound too like anxious foot-tapping, strangers
impatient to leave with
                what they've come to collect.

Tracheotomy

The terrible thing was his coughing, as his throat tried to expel the machinery of its breathing hole: Foam erupted, tinged with pink.

—Donald Hall on James Wright's last days

Obviously, I understand why he put it that way—
it must be disgusting to see
a loved one's body turning itself out

like that, but not to me—
it's my small son's proud survival
against a body not built

to work, or built then irreversibly
broken, irreversible as our guilt, before
he could ever use it.

Life, I've learned, can cling
to a certain amount of plastic,
and love is the things I do over

and over again—cleaning excess
secretions from my son's
lungs with a ten-inch catheter,

pouring liquid food down the tube
to his guts, cuing up the same
damn movie, holding his hand, soft

as tracing paper, and laughing
with him at the jokes I think
he makes. I was made

to be good like this, a father
before I was done being my father's
son. Lord, or reader, we have

suffered, and are ever suffering,
but it is not now of sadness
or pity I sing.

Video Baby Monitor

We can't give up watching
Cal through the night, through

the glassy fog of a little
screen, X-ray vision

piercing the skin of the dark.
He is seven, ever unsafe,

no baby, my baby, my son.
Already, the camera on

Simone broke, she's three,
and we won't replace it.

But Cal is different, his health
as tricky as wisdom, possessed

only by not knowing.
The monitor lies. I have been

here before, wrote this
before, am here now in these

very words. A watched
pot never boils, so perhaps

a son on a screen never
dies. Like the eyes

of a painting this image
follows wherever we move.

Surveillance is love, love
is every moment the last.

Barely moving picture, memory
of now, sleep, be still, be

safe. Night is long, life short.
I cover you with my eyes.

Centering

The first question is not how
to *accept* the premise that I
am not the subject of this day—
its focus, protagonist, star—
but how to *verify* it. Most
evidence suggests the opposite:
everything radiating in circles
from my head, for instance,
centering me amidst countless
concentric orbits, the dark side
behind me, the bright one ahead,
the hemisphere of memory meeting
the hemisphere of expectation
at a line that bisects me
at the point from which I look. Yes,
it is hard to explain, but I see
indications that my children
were born to teach me hope and
fear and selflessness or about
the many playthings there are;
and my mother died so I would
grow inured and sad ahead
of all my losses and disappointments
so as not to be surprised
or crestfallen; and my father
drank so I could walk away then
and I drink so I can walk away now.
It's almost obvious there *is* cause
and effect, logic, events
lining up with their morals,
like how my wife was presented
to me so I could learn to be good
to her, and bad. Perhaps
there are other things I'll be

meant to do. Everywhere I walk
I'm at the center of each step,
aligning sidewalk and sky like a
spirit-level-bubble and bringing along
as much of the world as matters.

The Hairdryer Cord Is All Tangled

You've stepped out of the shower,
dragged the towel up and down
your clean little self. Now

you've got to dry your hair, and quick.
Except there's this tangle. A clogged
artery? But nothing prevents you from

plugging it in—why won't you? *Does*
somebody love us all? Undo it,
or else who will, and when?

A time machine and God's eyes–that's what
you need. Does no one feel
the tectonic plates, magma, glaciers sliding?

You do, who've been anticipating death
since you were four. Your hair is still
so wet. Stop thinking! Your face

will stay that way like Gramma warned.
You'll catch your own swift undoing.
Untangle the cord, or the knots

will keep seething like a cracked oil pipe
snaking along the ocean floor.
This may be your one chance to stop

the fateful flap of the butterfly's wings.
Cities are shaking, sinking, singing.
The Earth is burning! Quick, untangle it!

Why Poetry: A Partial Autobiography

I could not learn
to become
my mother for obvious
reasons that were not obvious

to me, so I waited. I felt
as incorrect
playing baseball
as a bear cub moving in

with a family of turtles.
Other boys
sensed my fear

of them and, I now think,
were afraid
they were overlooking something
that should have

scared them: themselves.
I was always afraid of myself,

my mind, quite clearly a dangerous
place: I could think

about anything, any
horrible, depraved thing, and

whether or not I *did*
at that tender age, I knew
I was not safe
in my head, which was

where I knew my self was.
Childishly, I assumed

only *my* head was like that,
that they hated me
for an accurate, intuitive
reason. In fact,

I now think, they knew
better and hoped

that by attacking
and shaming the fear
resident in me,

in *my* self, they might
drive away the dark
within theirs.

Instead they expressed it
which I did not,

hence I was a good candidate
for poetry

into which one's latent
monstrousness can seep

like moisture into good wood
for decades, a lifetime.
My monstrousness is rotting harmlessly now
in my poetry.

TWO

Why Poetry: A Partial Autobiography

It's about to rain, suddenly
and without mercy.
          The rain will be brief, I can tell,

but I will be driven inside within earshot

of those anxious sounds bent
on occluding my mind
          like a pile of unpaid bills

—perhaps I will even see the pile of bills.
The rain will be brief, but no matter—I won't

get back outside tonight.

  ~

So, I have maybe ten minutes

for this to get said
before all is wet and after the fact

  ~

because I have only a succession
of chances,
          most missed.

  ~

Cal is finally fast asleep; the machine
that makes the mist that keeps
his trach moist rattles like an idling truck.

Simone is plotting something, standing and yelling
in her crib, jumping now,
                                    her sleep a bad joke.

Ten years since last I was alone.
My mind is not my own.

~

Reading the new poems tonight of my old teacher
—she was never taken with me, not
particularly—I admire her lifelong pursuit

of childhood
through art.

She has pursued art as though
it is as serious as childhood,
which we all pursue to the end.

~

And yet, if her poems—ornate as stained glass
leaning against a wall in the glass shop, windows
looking in on almost
                            nothing—say anything,

it is, *I am alone; beauty is everything*
except company, so beauty is nothing, almost.

~

Does she want what I have? Do I? My poems
lie.

The rain is coming. A few drops more and I'll lose
these letters. Simone still won't sleep.

Nest

Simone is babbling to her nighttime friend,
a small pink fabric square,
while Cal gracefully

waves himself to sleep, smoothing his hands
across the bed, the air, his chest
like someone learning
to make spiderweb.

Slow is the quality of his motion, deliberate
as his brain instructs
his unheeding body.
How can one

heed? And Simone, under the sign
of perfection, lurches and jerks
toward whatever beckons her attention:
movement in impassioned fits, irregular

as heartthrobs, unlike Cal, the thread
of him continuously
unfurling, furling
again, some

verb with no word. You love your children
as much as anything
you were unprepared for:
fiercely, with fear,

with all the fucking hatred it takes.

Why Poetry: A Partial Autobiography

How tense it makes me, reading
poetry, knowing how much I miss, misunderstand,
how only some of the words
resolve under my eyes
                                into sentences
while others slip by unnoticed,
like a note inscribed on a greeting card
by an aunt who never knew me well.
What I mean is the job is never
done, I'm never through. And I'm not made
for tasks that linger; some
of me is always considering
all the money I owe
to banks and credit card companies
and the kid
                    who kindly bought
me most of my high school lunches
because my dad forgot to send me to school
with a couple of bucks.
                                Which is of course to say
reading poetry is a metaphor.
Nothing ever
finishes.

~

So why did I choose poetry?
Maybe because it acknowledges right away
what scares me most,
how the line breaks before
the thought is done, how the line,
a partial thing,
is the measure,
and it's never enough. My

          college love
never did come running back
after I sent her
that photocopied pamphlet
of heartbroke verses,
          and my lamentation
did not un-injure my son or
get me back my job.

~

I woke up panting and confused
from the same nightmare over and over
through childhood—I can't remember when
it stopped: my task was to build
with colored blocks atop
          a floating green
island a kind of little city;
this was urgent—there would be no
forgiveness if it was not complete.
The dream ended
          with me standing before
this hovering shard of land
as it hovered away,
my job still undone, and I was
dropped back into my bed to
beg my mother
          for something she could
understand but not give.

It's hard now not to see it as
a premonition, maybe a preparation
for her dying only a few years
later, her life, my life
like all lives, unfinished.

And so I came to poetry.

Apprehension

1
You can't prove it but

2
this is reality. It feels like

3
looking from within

4
a helmet, the air outside

5
unbreathable, unreachable, or

6
poisonously oxygen-rich, teeming,

7
fatally alive. There's no way

8
to know. The ones you can

9
ask you can't trust, and

10
the ones you can trust

11
don't answer. So you

12
accept the uncertainty in your guts,

13
vow to believe your

14
senses, and call the small terror

15
that accompanies all of it a symptom

16
of beauty or boredom or awe,

17
and so you step as if from

18
a cocoon with each footfall

19
along the sidewalk in front

20
of your apartment toward

21
the subway, another day of

Where Am I?

How far from what
                  I keep calling
the world?

It appears right here, a hand's
reach away, but
               it's miles and miles from

here to the end of my arm.

In the Waiting Room

magazines from a lost month litter the end
tables. A pretty nurse

pops her head in and says,
The doctor will see you now, though not

to you, and no one stands up—you are
the only one waiting.

But soon the doctor will cast the long shadow
of his diagnosis. You've got

a thorn in your paw, a toothache, chronic
wide eyes, fear of fear

of fear itself, time on your hands
slipping between your fingers,

lost lust, purgatory, online pain, short
straws, overexaggeration,

the tendency to list: short, fat, and forlorn,
ever inoperable . . . O to have

a nurse of your very own, a time-angel, someone
on the one and only payroll

to pass you the pill it's always time to take, whose
rear your eyes can follow

to Happytown. But now, here, however,
you are skimming an article

about the viral video that sank New York,
then a profile of the man

who played the real-life Michael Jackson.
An article on who really profits

from most chilly wind. On the truth about
close friendship. On ten safe things

to open your mind to. You are an
Elizabeth! You are one of *them*!

Soon someone will call you in.

THREE

Book Review: The Mountain Lion *by Jean Stafford*

Spoiler alert: in this all-but-forgotten
masterwork, Jean Stafford—who was once
widely regarded as the leading novelist

of her generation, and who wrote
this perverse, short,
lyrical novel, her second, during

the flailing failings
of her marriage to my hero
Robert Lowell—kills

Molly, her child-alter ego,
a girl too unloved and unloving
to survive puberty, too

pure and awful—like Stafford, who died
pickled and childish three
decades later after winning

the Pulitzer with her devastating,
hurtfully compassionate *Collected
Stories*—for this or any other world,

especially the necessarily
allegorical one of fiction.
I am broken now, hopeless; hope

is proved by this book to be
a contrivance. I have just
read the last pages in which

Molly's brother, Ralph—who,
to live, cannot love
either, has no spare love—shoots

her, aiming for the wild mountain
lion whose stuffed corpse
was to be the triumph

of his new manhood. I don't
hate Ralph—how can I, a boy,
mistaken, like me? And can I hate

Molly, who so needed Ralph
and everyone, still young enough to savor
the bittersweet of her anger?

What about Stafford, who hurt
herself, all our selves, with
this ending, her classic tragedy, writing,

decades later, *Poor old
Molly! I loved her dearly
and I hope she rests in peace.*

Fuck insight and analysis:
my heart is shot. Why
did she have to die? Why does

anyone? Why do you, do I?
Because of what Ralph was
feeling just before he accidentally

slaughtered the future? This book
must have ravaged the already
sleepless poet Gregory Orr,

who shot his brother, too, and
suffers that endless error
in poetry and prose. And because Molly

refused everything, she stood between
Ralph and tomorrow. But he grew, he
changed. Confused? Read

the book. In novels
people die because of what they *feel*.
In life, people die when

their bodies conk out,
exhausted machines that living
expends. And what

happens when people feel
their feelings in life?
Nothing? Anything? Brenda,

dear Brenda, my love, nothing
happens, I'm afraid. I'm sorry. And afraid.
A small breeze born in the heart

gently bends a blade of grass
and no one hears a word.
No one reads Stafford anymore—I asked

on Facebook. Stafford died, her
legacy gently dispatched
into the low air. O, life

is terrible, literature
ridiculous. Stafford's prose,
teeming and rich as loam,

could take Famous Franzen's
for a walk, feed it biscuits.
But who cares? Who remembers?

O, to have been Jean Stafford,
in the past I idealize, when the world
was less self-conscious, less

precise. I could be
dead already, warmish
beneath a blanket of dust. Joyful

are the faded, the once-greats
whose afterlives slipped out
a hole in posterity's pocket:

they are loved poignantly by
a needy few. O, to be kept
cozy in the bosoms of those

desperate and proud, forgotten
for all the good I do. Love
is sunlight streaming unevenly

through the canopy of leaves
overhead. We can only grow
in the brighter patches below, fading

where light is thin. Molly,
we are with you, nowhere and gone.
Mostly we are forgotten, too.

FOUR

Self-Portrait as the Man I've Become

When did I grow so
fastidious? When did I learn
to use spreadsheets? There was no
particular day; it happened in my
thirties, that mostly pleasant path
between youth and whatever's up next.

Two deer appeared suddenly in our
backyard today; I practically yelled
everyone to the window. They ate
leaves from our rented trees
and soon moved on. Simone
was amazed, Cal smiled. When
did the deer visit our yard?
It was sometime in my thirties.

Letters to Brenda

1

I'm so alone and sad and away.
We said we'd write so here
goes. As if, addressed
to you from this distance,
I could reveal something neither
of us knows when we're side by
side by side. As if love were
the frame that reveals the two
people in it. I like that:
"as if," which is making a
statement by taking it back.

2

It's hard to do anything when
there's no need: the leaves won't
go brown in spring if I don't write.
Will you weep if I leave
the blank page blank? I'm nervous
I'll say the right thing the wrong
way. But here I am, the long
white road before me. I envision
you at the end of it, period.

3

Should a love letter reveal
the lover to the beloved?
Should it recall me to you,
send me your way without

my having to leave where I am?
Or should it deliver you here,
my longing wrapping your shape,
your soft smooth skin and your
surprisingly long fingers in
the text where anyone can see
you and feel you as I do? We should
meet here, pulling these lines
over our bodies like a cool
sheet, cozy under the reader's gaze.

4

When I die I'll want you by my
bedside to hold my hand. Life
lasted decades and we outlived
our losses, never a good match but
no one else could have lived this.
I'll want to die first so you
can do this for me, though you'll
want to die first too. It's not
selfish to want to be said goodbye
to. Let's not argue. Let's both die
first together, each of us sitting
by each other's bedside where we
each lay gently expiring, explaining.

5

Imagine this is the surface
of a rippling pond—we are not
dying in this one—and you look
down and see my face where
your reflection should be. Would you
assume, then, that looking up

I see you instead of myself?
Love asks questions like this
with no hope of an answer.

6

We've promised to talk on the
phone—I am longing for your
voice as if it could hold me.
But what if one of us is not
in the mood? What if there's
nothing to say? It's easy
to feel like the other is
merely in the way. I'd be able
to hear the anger in your eyes.

7

Maybe it's generosity that lets us
each see the other instead of ourselves
in the pool: could I bear how I must
sometimes look to you, when I'm
angry or childish? Or, worse,
when you feel the full bloom
of your love for me—could I lock
eyes with the person you're
seeing then? I'm no match for him.

8

If I could slip you into my skin
and step out, for just a minute, let you
look out from behind my eyes, watch my
thoughts spinning inside your head,

let you feel the weight of my limbs
and my chest and my gut pulling down,
heavy with my little burdens, or rarer, lifting
upward with inner light, you'd have
everything you'd need to forgive me
and you and everyone everything.

9

It's been raining here all day.
Gray fills my insides like sleep.
I crave sunlight through leaves, which
promises its own faraway origin,
where beauty isn't surprising.
I don't want to spend my life
tiptoeing toward the next.

10

Words try to promise meaning
beyond what they say, as though
each one were a step on a path
to a distant outpost where, on a
wooden table, the final, simple
answer has been ruggedly carved.
Having gone there and attained
that knowledge, of course, one
can never come back, which is why
all writing must be imprecise,
so that we don't have to
leave each other, ever, my lover.

Which Is the Best Part of the Day?

when you are
alone when the
kids are

asleep when
simone first wakes
when brenda and

you finally lie
down when you
fuck when you

wake in the middle
of the night and
realize you can

go back to sleep when
you are eating
when you are on the

way to work when cal
is smiling when you
have a full

plate of food when
the TV is on when
you can concentrate

on a book when
you masturbate
in the shower when

you are checking
things off when
your tea is ready

when cal settles
back down when you're
alone when you're not

Low Note

1

There is nowhere to begin.
I know nothing of rivers
except that this one seems soft
and kind from this distance.
I look everywhere for
kindness, a gentle, generous
reception for myself.
I was brought up to believe
the world should be fair, not
that I should have to make it so.

2

Tomorrow is our daughter's
second birthday, and I am
far away. We tell ourselves
she won't know the difference
when we celebrate in
two weeks, but
one never knows what sets
regret moaning, which
are the hooks that won't come out.

3

You will have been a good
mother, anxious
and angry at all that has
hurt us, saving your
joy in fascicles in drawers.

4

I feel today that even
if we manage to move
the heavy stone, it will
still be a stone, sitting
heavy in someone's path.
That's nothing to teach
our children, though
could it have been something
my father once said?

5

In a plain mood like this
nothing looks like much more
than it is. That too
is nothing to teach, though
it may be close to the truth.

6

Magic ebbs away like time
ticking into a bucket.
Sometimes it blooms
momentarily again,
a sunset or whatever
draws milk back out
of the earth. I could
teach our children that
and let them find their own
disappointments.

7

I can try to teach our children
not knowing what they will
remember, a cold stare one
night an all-but-permanent
lesson and words little more
than fading bells. My father
once seized my arm in anger.
He was mostly kind, but
I never forget that small nut of pain.

8

The worst of me, screaming
your name like drawing
a little knife, is no less true
than the good husband I wish
you'd record in a poem.
It seems silly tonight to ask
that we celebrate the full
circle our cruelty makes
where it meets our calm.

9

A bird cuts harshly
through the gray sky, an emblem
in a language I strain
to recognize, pretend
to know some words in. The work
of life that is done at home,
I think, is mostly undone.

10

There is nowhere to end
either, except on a low
note, or so tonight
would have it, no knowing
for us what the reason is.

All Elegies

The past gathers itself quickly like debris;
time eddies around it, sort of stays put.
It takes fewer years than it took.
Dorothea is dead, just shy of one hundred

and one. Richard is old and only growing older,
though many of the greats of his great
generation are already decades dead.
Chris is dead, old then, when we passed

eventless afternoons unpacking boxes
in a tobacco shop. I was just out of college.
He was too old to be hauling out
trash, but too proud to let me.

Michael Jackson is dead. Even
Michael? Was he ever even alive?
Just yesterday a friend told me
his friend had hanged himself

at twenty-three, too young
not to hope for response or revenge.
I make myself sound old, but I'm not.
Of course, my mother is dead, gone

half as long as she lived, longer
than we were alive together. My father
is still alive, so I'm from somewhere.
Both the children of his second wife

have just had children, and I have two, too.
We diminish as we multiply.
But like Delmore says, *I am I.*
Memories can't account for everything.

A dead bird by the playground
was shoveled away. Last night I stomped
out the life of a quarter-sized wasp.
I put the kids to bed. I did the dishes.

I threw out Brenda's blackened roses.
Eventually, time passes, but it eddies,
like seeing someone again by surprise
after exchanging drawn-out goodbyes.

Tomorrow and Tomorrow Again

Of course I don't know what
happens to us: if we survive in the
hands of love; if Cal, if Simone
and all the trembling answers
those questions entail; whether
by time or by disease or by
an atom bomb right in the eye. Is it
possible death could be thrilling
and fun? And after could there be
something somewhere and what
will we do if we see each other
there? Will the same songs stay stuck
in our heads? Will medicine
succeed in making life so long
we will beg for medicine to end it?
One cannot lock eyes with a bird,
its eyes vacant as ball bearings, but
mustn't there be some recognition
in everything? Some fury, some
questioning? If one phrase could echo
throughout eternity, would the ear
on the other end return
a word? But what am I asking?
Will I ever see a whale, and will his size
compared to mine be a true
form of knowledge? Loneliness
has depths writing fails to fathom.
I could be clearer, say more, but
it wouldn't mean as much. Mother
will I ever find you again? Is fear
of spiders fair? Is a power
above minding the scales, be it
science or gods or the weather,
and can they be tipped toward

balance from here? Is beauty more
than another form of pleasure?
What, which, when, how is better?

Another Day

It should be difficult,
always difficult, rising
from bed each morning,
against gravity, against

dreams, which weigh
like the forgotten names
of remembered faces.
But some days it's

easy, nothing, to rise,
to feed, to work, to
commit the small graces
that add up to love,

to family, to memory,
finally to life, or
what one would choose
to remember of it, not

those other leaden
mornings when sleep
is so far preferable
to pulling over one's

head the wet shirt
of one's identity again,
the self one had been
honing or fleeing

all these years,
one's fine, blessed
self, one's only,
which another day fills.

Edgemont

Was it really so terrible,
those prism-perfect seasons, that place,
four-cornered and predictable, where I
learned to love sun dust

carousing in the rays slanting
through my childhood's gray
venetian blinds? True, everyone
was politely dying,

in undefiant decay behind
heavy ornamented doors
twice locked—there must have been
other husbands stewing beside my father

at South Seas Chinese Restaurant and Bar
instead of at home for family dinnertime.
Mom and I ate at the table, four places set,
with Mrs. Brown, whom we called our

housekeeper, but she raised me
and died sad and alone, perhaps beside
her mysterious daughters, long since
fired and with nothing from me

to show for her years—perhaps a few
of my kindergarten drawings. In childhood
we seed late-life's great regrets.
But I played outside for seventeen

years, no matter that place was
merely the set for a film about that place
no one would make. Of course my unhappiness
flourished there, molding in the damp

ironic spring, jealous of summer,
drying to a brown patch
in transcendent autumn, finding a kind of
company in old, interminable winter.

But wouldn't the halls have jaundiced
anywhere we lived? Maybe not,
maybe not, if my parents had been
more joyful, if they had chosen a town

with thinner walls, less-expansive
lawns, nearer neighbors. But people
die alive in apartments, too, communities
only as strong as their least

compassionate families. So much of that life
happened behind doors, evenings,
loved ones doing things other than
talking. Daytime was barren, the kids

all sequestered into one of two
schools, public but small and funded
like private academies by high taxes
on all our luxurious properties.

Between eight and three, the town belonged
to stay-at-home moms, who oversaw
the ornamentation of vast front yards
and sometimes helped out

in their children's second-grade classrooms—
my mom did one spring, and I woke
like each of those Fridays was my
birthday. But what did the other mothers

do all week? Jerry worked, like my mother—
Jerry was a teacher. I don't think Folly

did—and those were their real names!
Also Bernice, Sherry, Rona . . . they were

the Nadlers, the Rubensteins, the Breshers,
mostly second-generation European Jews
who'd made good on the promises
of their parents' hard-earned poverty

having moved this ambitious distance from
the boroughs of New York City. It sounds,
I know, like I'm merely spinning stereotype,
but this was my home—it was true!

This is what the successful offspring
of Holocaust survivors did,
after depositing their parents in Florida
(my grandmother lived there, we visited

at least once a year). This was the 1980s.
There was money and hope that
hadn't yet run out in our temporary
home built to negotiate with doubt.

Like everywhere else, childhood
lasted forever, miles and miles
of time between yearly checkups.
The day after my birthday, no

next birthday in sight. Days
were lives, ending and beginning,
all deaths and births and TV specials.
Think of all the bugs I met

in the dirt in front of my house.
I can't recall the last time I sat
cross-legged, digging the ground
with a stick. I was no different from anyone.

Of course school days singed my guts
like slow branding irons. I knew
all the corners and back roads too well
to lose my virginity there, so I kept it until

I could leave. How lonely that made me,
but most people are lonely, and
young time seems always to be
running out while taking forever

to pass. I recall my sense of it
passing, thick air in empty rooms.
Nothing's so poignant now as then,
and mostly I'm relieved.

We might have been happier, but
my parents weren't bred
for idle joy by their fallen Jewish families,
those schools of half-hearted compromise.

He drank and ran like his father had.
She worked and made do like her mother.
Though she was extraordinary in her way.
She was, after all, the president

of the recruiting firm she and my dad
co-owned. They found jobs
for 1980s marketing execs, back when
they handed out those jobs like business cards.

It all went to ruin when she died
in '94. It all went to ruin, but it had
long been on its way. My generation
was taught there was nothing immoral

about sex, it was merely lethal.
Then there was the first President Bush,

the first Iraq war. Soon enough
no one was hiring execs

anymore. They fired Mrs. Brown—
she died to me right then, but kept calling,
creepy and despondent, begging me to beg
my dad for money throughout high school,

my own interminable gauntlet. But I wasn't different.
One teacher to whom I bragged about my shaved
head and eager high school beard
countered flatly: *Craig, you're not that weird.*

And there *was* love and joy—
there had always been. My mom
was fun, my dad sort of funny, and
I never doubted, despite my misery,

that I belonged to a normal, happy
family. Later I learned to blame them
for my ghosts and weight problem, but
not then. Every New Year

the three of us would huddle together
around the living room chair, taking turns
wearing a festive hat with a
feather—they must have picked it up

at some party years back—taking
family pictures by the fancy miracle
of a new camera with a timer
on the shutter. My father would hurry

across the room, the camera suddenly
ticking, as if to catch the soon-to-be
immortal moment. He made it every time,
though where are those pictures now?

More paper, the lost manifest of my memory,
boxes and file cabinets stored someplace
four homes hence, which promises,
someday, to verify what I think I felt.

An eighteenth-century stone wall ringed
my yard and those on my block, one
of many relics of the tenant farms—
subjects of the great manor house, now

a tourist attraction, a few miles up
the Hudson. The three oldest
houses in Edgemont—which was once
quaintly Greenville (my elementary school

was given our town's former
name)—had stood since the 1700s,
with barns or pillared porches or
wooden fences to set them apart

from the stucco or clapboard abodes
that had overrun all the roads, which were
named after our first families—
the Underhills, the Seeleys—

whose generations lay buried in sizable
plots in the old graveyard behind
my high school track, whose church
had been replaced by a Burger King

and a tiny mall with no good stores.
I spent hours by those graves, trying
to fathom time, I looked
into that charged dirt for

the past returning like my reflection
on a pond. I spent my afternoons

smoking by a pond, man-made,
that opened below one of those immemorial

mansions. I ran my hand over stones
some two-hundred-years-dead
man had set into a wall to mark
the edge of his land, and the past

seemed less distant because I did.
I could hold that rock
and rewind time and find myself
standing between verb tenses.

It *wasn't* so bad, was it? Nor
so long ago. Twenty years can fit
neatly in the snow globe of one
small thought. And yet, already I talk of

that past as *the* past, and finally
I think it is. But who really wants
to hear about it? Where's all
the poetry, one wonders. Not there

in the thin and dwindling mythology
of another middle-class family.
I've wished the hell that made me
looked more like Hell, some darkly

broken faraway out of whose muck
I could have arisen. But the days were
gorgeous in spring and summer,
sweetly nostalgic in fall. In winter,

there was always good snow to throw.
Children opened like soft dandelions
in all those landscaped yards.
Our seeds blew wide and most of us have grown

prosperous—we have money now
and safe, smart kids of our own.
I was raising mine in the city, a few
long miles from that lush suburban trap,

thinking, from thirty minutes away,
I was free to never go back. And now,
because my kids deserve some grass
of their own to hunt for bugs in,

my wife and I have put our money down
on a little house in New Jersey
in another happy town
like Edgemont. May our years pass gently.

Gnostic

I have a soul, I know it, have always
recognized it there within
me like a luminous ball in the dark

between my heart
and my liver, shifting
around under my ribs,
expressing itself sometimes

where my ribcage closes
just beneath the skin, a pushing
outward of something song-like, light-like
that could almost lift me
up and out of myself through myself

knowing everything I know and much more.
Fear—extreme fear—was part of it,
and something eons beyond
excitement, a certainty
that the body was only a beginning.

It was what I knew childhood
was for, to live close
to this, to sense it often, daily,
not to seek it—because

I was terrified of it, correctly—
but to accept it; it was
obvious, undeniable, like rain
or the hard floor of the house
if I tripped and fell.

I say this now, surely,
with a kind of nostalgia, with longing.

Life is much more literal
thirty years later. Transcendence
is mostly replacing one screen with another.
All light is fairly dim. There is nothing

to frighten me but death and debt.
And yet, that other, better terror
still rings—I hear it—between
and beneath these words.
Why else am I writing them?

Another Poem on My Daughter's Birthday

There must be soft words
for an evening like this, when the breeze
caresses like gentle fingertips
all over. I don't know

how not to write darkly and sad.
But it's five years today since
my little girl was born, cut safely
from the noose.

We meant nothing but hope;
how near death is to that.

Only children, only some children,
get to run free from these snags. She
was born! She lived and she grows
like joy spreading from the syllables

of songs. She reminds me of now
and now and now.
                          I must learn
to have been so lucky.

Acknowledgments

Thanks to the editors of the publications below, in which some of these poems appeared, sometimes in different versions:

A Public Space: "Apprehension";
Atlas Review: "Which Is the Best Part of the Day?," "Why Poetry: A Partial Autobiography ('It's about to rain . . .')";
Bennington Review: "Edgemont";
Colorado Review: "Free";
Denver Quarterly: "Another Day";
Gulf Coast: "Low Note," "Self-Portrait Beside Myself";
The Mackinac: "Self-Portrait as the Man I've Become";
New American Writing: "Why Poetry: A Partial Autobiography ('How tense it makes me . . .')";
The New Republic: "Where Am I?";
The Paris Review: "Book Review: *The Mountain Lion* by Jean Stafford," "Why Poetry: A Partial Autobiography ('I could not learn . . .')";
PEN Poetry Series: "Tomorrow and Tomorrow Again";
Poetry International: "Gnostic," "The Hairdryer Cord Is All Tangled";
Prairie Schooner: "Night Nurse";
T: The New York Times Style Magazine: "Video Baby Monitor";
Tin House: "All Elegies," "Tracheotomy";
Women's Studies Quarterly: "Nest."

"Another Poem on My Daughter's Birthday" appeared in Poem-a-Day, sponsored by the Academy of American Poets on Poets.org.

"Why Poetry: A Partial Autobiography ('I could not learn . . .')" also appeared in the anthology *The Unprofessionals: New American Writing from the Paris Review.*

Thank you to Gibson Fay-LeBlanc, Gabriel Fried, Rusty Morrison, Nick Twemlow, Robyn Schiff, and Rachel Zucker, and of course, Brenda, for lavishing generous attention on these poems.

And Brenda gets a second special thank you: these poems track some wild years, my love, don't you think?

Enduring gratitude to Purcell Palmer and all at the Catwalk Institute for time, space, and kindness in which this book took shape.

About the Author

Craig Morgan Teicher is the author of two previous books of poetry: *Brenda Is in the Room and Other Poems*, winner of the 2007 Colorado Prize for Poetry; and *To Keep Love Blurry*; as well as *Cradle Book: Stories and Fables*. He is the editor of *Once and for All: The Best of Delmore Schwartz*. He is a prolific book critic, writing regularly for *The New York Times, The LA Times*, NPR, and other venues. He has taught at NYU, the University of Iowa Writers' Workshop, Princeton, and elsewhere, and lives in New Jersey with his wife, the poet Brenda Shaughnessy, and their children.

BOA Editions, Ltd.
American Poets Continuum Series

Colophon

BOA Editions, Ltd., a not-for-profit publisher of poetry and other literary works, fosters readership and appreciation of contemporary literature. By identifying, cultivating, and publishing both new and established poets and selecting authors of unique literary talent, BOA brings high-quality literature to the public. Support for this effort comes from the sale of its publications, grant funding, and private donations.

⊡   ⊡   ⊡

The publication of this book is made possible, in part, by the support of the following patrons:

Anonymous
Gwen & Gary Conners
Steven O. Russell & Phyllis Rifkin-Russell

and the kind sponsorship of the following individuals:

Jenna & Steve Fisher
Jere Fletcher
Sandi Henschel
X.J. & Dorothy M. Kennedy
Jack & Gail Langerak
Boo Poulin
Deborah Ronnen & Sherman Levey
Steven O. Russell & Phyllis Rifkin-Russell
Alfred J. Sciarrino, Esq.
Sue Stewart, *in memory of Stephen L. Raymond*
Lee Upton, *in memory of Lana Upton Kaltz*
Michael Waters & Mihaela Moscaliuc